T0128719

# STARTING

## *Over*

### ALLEY M

authorHOUSE®

*AuthorHouse™*
*1663 Liberty Drive*
*Bloomington, IN 47403*
*www.authorhouse.com*
*Phone: 1 (800) 839-8640*

*Published by AuthorHouse    04/25/2016*

*ISBN: 978-1-5246-0529-2 (sc)*
*ISBN: 978-1-5246-0528-5 (e)*

*Library of Congress Control Number: 2016906700*

*Print information available on the last page.*

# Table of Contents

## LOVE ZONE

## DANGEROUS PASSIONS

## THE OTHER SIDE OF ME

## HER STORY OF A BROKEN HEART

# LOVE ZONE

## Angel Sleep

She's an angel asleep
So quiet
With the heavens in her face
Dreams
Take her mind into space
No expression is there
Her lips are still
There is no sound
You want to awake her
Look into her eyes
So full of the earth
Yet you don't want to disturb the dance
That is
A body never laid so still
She is an angel
Asleep
Forever.

-       Alley M.

## *Calm*

Your voice
R
A
I
N
S
D
O
W
N
On me
  Like sunshine

  Oh I miss you so
        Though at times
       You could
         Work my last nerve
        You deserve
          Every ounce of love

Blue skies
  Above
      Oh how I await
      Your supple kisses
Our sly tristes
    Oh how I submit
     To the man in
    You.

                     – Alley M.

### Kind of Temptation

Mysterious eyes
Staring into abyss
What kind of temptation is this?
Heart racing
Smiles in ties
What kind of temptation is this?
Tongues slip
Traces of honey
Across lips
Only in the imagination
Cuz what we facing
Got us patiently waiting
Mysterious eyes
Entwined in mines
Pictured it 1000 times
Where does your path lead?
Plant your seeds
Of intelligence
Ambition I can't miss
Hands trace
Hips
Mysterious eyes
Staring into abyss
What kind of temptation is this?

- Alley M

## Passion

Passion of the pen
Passion as we touch again
I love your sin
Strokes of rhythms
To the heart beat
Sweet sweeps of lips
Your sugar engulfs me.

- Alley M.

## Smile

That brilliant smile
Oh that brilliant smile
What did I ever do to deserve
Its grace
Never a tear drop in its place
Oh sweet honey do
Oh how it becomes you
Ear to ear length
White as a blanket of snow
Dimples
The sparkle of a star
To what do I owe
This amazing treat
To bestow my presence
At your feet?

- Alley M.

## Solace

Sunshine
Booms
Flowers
Sweet scent
Abreast your neck
Glossy glaze
Over your eyes
As you gaze into mines
In you I find solace
Pitter patter of heart
Beats
Meet
As your chest presses
Against mines
I gleam upon
Starry skies
In my room
As I melt into you
Softest skin I've ever known
Precious kisses
Of golden drops.

- Alley M.

## Spirit Journey

Is it safe to say
You took my hand today
Whisked me away
To a new journey?
Sneaky whisps
Brush upon my ear
Passion that I've never known
As fantasies bloom
In a dark room
Songs we agreed upon
Engulfs us
As we connect
Through lyrics
That tell the tales we can not
Express
Heaves of chests
Syncopate
Celestial souls
Do a fiery dance
Of romance.

- Alley M.

## Stallion

Chocolate
Sips
Of a Hershey fountain
Thor
Stands before me
Haughty
And mighty
Pebble skin
Washed by the ocean
Dark almond eyes
Warrior
Let your heartbeat
Be my lullaby
White-bottomed
Feet from sand
I can hear
The waves crash
In the background
As I crash into you
Spectacular starbursts
Arise
From your eyes
The bliss
Of cool breeze
As whimpers

And woes
Of love
Send spinal surges
And
Tingly curly toes
On neurological
Journeys
You've awoken
My third eye.

- Alley M.

# DANGEROUS PASSIONS

## Cute Addiction

Smile
Cutie come here
What's ya name?
Mr. Mr.
Kiss ya
Wom-an good bye
Curly hair
Light brown eyes
I despise
Pink lips
Gifts give
What I take
Smile
Cutie go there
Abandon your shell
Unveil the mask
Get freaky
Tall handsome thang you
Voice
Clouds spread
Hear thunder
Erase my blunder
Take me under
Ya sheets
Beat the batter
Cutie with that bootie
You coming my way
Baby say hi

I have to have this guy
Muscles pulsing
Like that
Heart beat-
ing inside
of him
inside of me
skin ain't light
ain't dark
game ain't wrong
ain't right
last night
brother held me tight
outta sight
held me down
with hospitality
the morning brang me back
to reality
mental causality
regarding to your actions
smile
cutie share
your wealth
under ya belt
what I felt
was meant for you
noting intentional
that it came to me
tell me if you want me to
dedicate myself to you

combine
in heat
arrive in defeat
but I have to have this guy
shy timid
me
out going
him
opposites
us
attract
never take back
your luck
smile
cutie
come here
what's your name
mr. mr.
kiss ya
woman goodbye.

- Alley M.

## Panther

Subtle
She stalks
Heels
The paws
When she walks
Night prowl
She's out to devour
If ever you cross her path
She locks you
Into her hypnosis
With glowy eyes
And with panting breath
She lures.

- Alley M.

## Seduction

Your whispers
They smooth me
Really and truly
To the depth
Of eternity
Can I glide into your body?
You subdue me
As I follow your commands
Lips brush against cheeks
Sapping up soul
Slowly absorbing my
Weak
State
Hands hook onto arms
For brace
As you take me on this journey.

- Alley M.

# THE OTHER SIDE OF ME

## Day Dreamer

I am a day dreamer
You see me at anytime
& look into my eyes
Notice that I am in a different
Futuristic galaxy
Holographic
Yet no one can see through me
I'm on a journey
A different path
Can you do the math?
I am an equation
Come on, try to figure me out
Because I know without a doubt
That I am going off into another dream
I fantasize about luxuries
Red carpets, paparazzi, magazine covers, tours and
All the different countries
I wish for better understanding
And greater emotional strength
I'm hell bent
And what was sent to me
Was the reality
Of
Dreams
And all things in between
I dream about
Cures
For pandemics, epidemics, viruses

And hereditary diseases
My imagination
Does as it pleases
What's my thesis?
"Sweet dreams are made of these"
Half emotion, half fantasy
Day dream to get away
From another drawn out day
There's not much I can say
To describe this way
Of life
I dream of being a wife
Dream about what would've happen if I
Had used that butcher's knife
That night
I'd probably be behind bars
Day dream about becoming a star
Owning my own sports car
With tricked out details
Dream about owning a retail store
I dream for more
Dream to become better
And to whether through the stormy weather
I dream of getting my act together
I dream of that letter
That's going to give me my big break
I dream to learn from
My mistakes
I dream to escape
Escape pain,
Stress,
And all the rest
That comes along with being seventeen

I dream of being a queen
I dream to take me back
I dream about laying down tracks
I dream that one day
I can watch my paper stack
Sit back & just laugh
'cause you did the math
To the equation at hand
And realized that a day dreamer
Is just who I am.

- Alley M.

*Devil in a Blue Dress*

They call me devil
In a blue dress
He calls me empress
He doesn't know yet
How mischievous
I could be
You see
I have a whole
Other side of me
She's methodological
In seduction
Suction of soul
Vampire-ish
In how she feels
Off of body language
Cunning
And stunning
Epitome of beauty
Her survival
Is your blood.

- Alley M.

# Dream

It's happening again
Beads of sweat
Heart thumping
Surrounded by darkness
Lost focus
Don't know
Which realm
I'm in
Heard gunshots again
I'm tripping
Terrors
Oppose beauty sleep
Saw a man following me
Thought his face
Looked vaguely familiar
Momentarily
I've met a killer
Seduction
Of psychosis
So sweet
I think I wanna get
Caught up

In this
Dream state
Damn I'm slipping
I'm going under
Ripping
Into the blunder
Of this nightmare.

- Alley M.

## Fraction of the Mind

A half
Mind alteration
Demanding altercations
Staggering illuminations
That I am awaiting.
A whole
Give me it all
Specialties and guarantees
That I am awaiting.
A third
Give me three
So I can see towards my goal
That I am awaiting.
A fourth
Mind stallin'
Thoughts crawling' the wall
'n' I've seen it all
That I am awaiting.
A quarter
Body language
It's not time yet
But I bet I'm ready

That I am awaiting.
A sixth
Body signing
It has wings
'n' believing in me
That I am awaiting.

- Alley M.

## Lily Fields

I dream of lily fields
In this concrete jungle
Hear the trains
Screech
And rumble
As they yearn on by
Out my window
Glass shattering
Basketballs thumping
Oh yeah
Its summertime
Think I'll head to the -
Corner store
Once more
I made about three trips
For the day already
Love the attention
They think I'm such
A pretty lady
But I still dream of
Lilly fields
In this concrete jungle
Youngn's
Running down each store
As they run down
Ice cream trucks

Asking each other
For a buck
O.G.'s on the corner
Betting on their luck
And still I dream
Of lily fields
In this concrete jungle
Damn I saw another
Cat fight today
Head wraps
Jay's and Uptowns
Ole project way
Got a sickening love
For the jungle
Where a cougar like I must roam
Still I wish to explore
Other thrones
Sweet breeze
Under palm trees
Crystals adorn
My mellow drink
If only...
Maybe one day
But for now
As I enter back
Into this over-priced third bedroom
Chopped up in weird ways
Sort of a bungle-low
As I lay in front

A cracked window
Tryna beat this heat
Staring at the ceiling
Man
I think my body
Kind of neat
All types of conceited I am
As I dream
Of lily fields
In this concrete jungle.

- Alley M.

## My Boyfriend?

You wanna be my boyfriend?
For what?
I know you don't have a crush on me
You think that game you spit
Can blind me?
Telling me lies
'bout how you want me
To birth your child
How you wanna walk down
That aisle with me
You wanna be my boyfriend?
For what?
I know you don't have a care
In the world for me
Except to be
The first one
To own my body
I don't understand
Why ya'll can't just
Be honest with a sista
Let me know
If it's only sex you want

I may be hurt
And disappointed
At first
But I'll get over it
You wanna be my boyfriend?
For what?
I know you don't have a care for me
Except to be
The first to rule my body.

- Alley M.

*Past*

In darkness
The past haunts
Regrets
Of bets
I always had to live on the wild side…
Right?
Must admit
It was fun
All those nights
On the run
Flighty friends
Had me
Like damn I trusted again…
Caught up
In stipulations
Amazing
I'm around
To tell the story
I've reveled

In indecent glory
Trophies
Of breaking rules
I just had to do
What everyone else was doing
Somber silence
As I talk to the only
Person
I know understands...
Me.

- Alley M.

*Suffocating*

These four walls
Closing in
Suffocating
Dying to win
Forced
To settle
For a level
To play with the devil
Queen rebel
I demise
Going with the status quo
Hate to be
Trapped in one place
If only I could get
A taste
Of the dreams
I dream so much.

- Alley M.

# HER STORY OF A BROKEN HEART

## Gray

Every time
I close my eyes,
I see your creamy grays
Staring back;
Piercing my soul.
Your eyes
Disturb my peace,
Terror causes me to awake at night,
Horror of a stalker,
I am not amused.
You fuel me to run,
To the end of the world
And never return.
Gray the color
Of my pity for you,
Your ownership of a queen victorious
Will the duke
Appreciate his lady
And take care of his castle
Or shall abandonment over come
Your weathering heart
And leave that cold apathetic stare
Of your cloudy grays in my memory?

- Alley M.

I don't want to say goodbye,
Because that means no more you.
I don't want to leave,
Because that means no more me.
I don't want to be alone,
Because that means no more us.
Don't leave this relationship in the dust;
We have potential to make it work.
I don't want to argue,
Because that means we aren't in love.
I don't want to fight,
Because I don't want to hurt.
I don't want to cry,
Because that means we're falling apart.
Don't neglect me,
We can solve this,
I don't want to say goodbye.

- Alley M.

## Love

Timing for me and you
Everything so synchronized
Tell me why
Everything we do
Is so connected
Are you my world
Am I yours?
Wanna be around 24/7
For what happens
Need you there
In the very same way
I can't go day by night
Crying
Because ya love
Escapes my heart
Disappears from my world
Tears of passion flare
Can you take me there?
Ecstasy for eternity?
How could something so special
In my life
Have such little impact
To me
And everything around us?
Tears will never stop flowing
If you never know
How I feel

- Alley M.

## Poison

Poison
Your love is poison
Your attitude is poison
Your personality is poison
Yet I'm so addicted
Like a crack fiend
On the ave
Can't get enough of how you feel
How you touch
But it's too much
Poison
Running through my vessels
Every time I look you in those cold eyes
Poison
In every inch from head to toe
From those braids
Right down to those sneakers
And everywhere in between
Poison
In every word you say
'cause every word you say is a lie
Poison
In every smile
'cause every smile is fake
Poison
Your name is poison
Poison
You are poison.

- Alley M.

Listen to the melody
And harmonies
Of the R&B song
As memories flood
My cubical
Fighting back the blood tears
Wiping away the sweet sweat
Visions of love
Escape my reaches
All is lost
Again as the songs
Screeches to a halt
My heart pounds
In connection to the chemistry
Another vibe
Bumps as I close my eyes
Seventy two hours awake
From the misery
Actions become ghosts in life
Every night
Haunting me
Never letting me forget
That R&B
Song that played
When our love
Was laid to rest.

– Alley M.

## Storm

Your voice
R
A
I
N
S
D
O
W
N
On me
Like **THUNDER**
Oh how I miss peace
Hard at times
You could be
Rock hard
Stone face
Arms in a X no place
For love

Stormy skies
Above
Oh how I await
Misogynistic freedom
Our devious combats
Oh how I submit
To the demon in you.

— Alley M.

*Tears of an Eagle*

No more whispers
Just a cold shiver
When the wind creeps
To my window
You are not next to me
There is no way on God's green earth that this could be
I thought love
Equaled eternity
Reality
Is so harsh
A tear
Shallow as your heart
Falls on my pillow
Where you used to lay
And if my eagle soul
Should ever die
At your presence
That is the very essence
Of life
Of love
At times when the minute
Passes the second
With the swift of a hand
You understand
I get restless
My body gets weak
And if love made its way
Back into this empty home

That acts as a house
No movement
Still
In the day
Creepy at night
Vast and dry
A drought
And make it alive again
Fast, quick and swift
With the fragrance of my soul
Amongst the midst
Of sanity
It will be then that the eagle
Sees
The lion returning to his pride.

- Alley M.

## Trust

Rags to riches
Burnt bridges
Due to accomplishments
Fake friends
Made death wishes
Venom kisses
Smiles at your misses
All while
Hands are stretched
Sleepless nights
That's your instincts
Haters hooked on
Still for the links
Trusted personnel stealing
Finances
Jet setters
Business class
You know...
The fancy suits
Reptilians worse than
Poison
Shape shifting
Shooting heroine
All what fame is about

All about the glam
Man...
All the fortune
Never found a piece of mind
Never any privacy
All the blood, sweat, tears
You see
Never meant anything
Welcome to the circus.

- Alley M.

Printed in the United States
By Bookmasters